FEDERAL BUREAU OF INVESTIGATION, UNITED S[T]

WASHINGTON, D.C.

MIRANDA V. ARIZONA

CURRENT ARREST OR REC

DATE ARRESTED OR RECEIVED	CHARGE OR OFFENSE (If code citation is used it should be accompanied by charge)
7-5-1963 MARICOPA COUNTY	COUNT I-KIDNAPPING COUNT II-RAPE (FIRST DEGREE) TO RUN CONCURRENTLY

OCCUPATION	RESIDENCE OF PERSON FINGERPRINTED
TRUCK DRIVER	WIFE: TWILA MIRANDA 157 E. COMMONWEL[L] CHANDLER, ARIZONA

If COLLECT wire reply or COLLECT telephone reply is desired, indicate here.

☐ Wire reply ☐ Telephone reply

Telephone number

CONTENTS

Miranda's Crimes

As it neared midnight on March 2, 1963, a man in his early 20s pulled his car out of a driveway in Phoenix, Arizona. The car almost hit a young woman walking down the street. The man stopped his car, stepped out of it, and approached the woman. Without warning, he reached out and grabbed her arm. With his other hand, he covered her mouth. He said:

Don't scream, and I won't hurt you.

For the woman, called Jane Doe to protect her identify, an evening of horror was about to begin. The man shoved her into his car and tied her hands and feet. As he ordered her to lie still, he placed a cold, sharp object against her neck. Then he drove into the desert outside Phoenix.

Jane Doe believed she should not risk her life by angering her abductor. She did not fight him when he attacked her. He committed rape, a crime he had attempted before with other women. Before taking Jane Doe back into the city, he demanded her money. She handed over all she had: $4.

Within a few hours, the Phoenix police were at Jane Doe's home. They asked her about the abduction. Over the next few days, they questioned her several more times. Jane Doe was 18 years old, but her relatives said that she had emotional problems that made her seem and act much younger.

In 1963, the Phoenix Police Department protected a rapidly growing city of about 450,000 people.

9

Jane Doe sometimes changed the facts of her story when she talked to the police. The police gave her a lie detector test, and she seemed to have lied several times. But Jane Doe insisted she had been assaulted. She said she knew she would recognize her abductor if she ever saw him again.

A week after the assault, Jane Doe was out late with a relative. They walked near the street where Jane Doe had been abducted. Jane Doe thought she saw a familiar green car—her abductor's car. Her relative wrote down the license plate number and brought it to the police. Using that clue, the police tracked down the owner of the car—a man named Ernesto Miranda—who also lived in Phoenix.

WHO IS JANE DOE?

In some legal cases, including ones involving rape or other forms of sexual assault, the name of the victim is not made public. In legal matters, Jane Doe and Barbara Roe are names commonly used to hide the real name and identity of a woman. John Doe is often used for men.

On March 13, Officers Carroll Cooley and Wilfred Young went to Miranda's home and took him to the police station. Miranda later said:

I didn't know whether I had a choice.

At the time, the officers did not charge Miranda with a crime. When he asked the police why they were taking him in, Young and Cooley did not answer. Even so, Miranda acted calmly during the car ride and showed no signs of worry or guilt.

Jane Doe identified Ernesto Miranda's car as the one belonging to her abductor.

At the station, the officers took Miranda to a tiny room. The police called it the sweat room, where they made people accused of crimes sweat with fear and anxiety—and, they hoped, confess to crimes. Miranda matched the description of a man wanted for another robbery, so Cooley and Young asked him about that crime as well as the rape of Jane Doe. Miranda denied a role in either crime.

In 1963, police officers in sweat rooms across the United States did whatever they could to win confessions. They tried to break down a criminal's resistance to their questions. In some cases, that meant playing "good cop, bad cop." Using this

11

strategy, one officer would yell at or hit a suspect, while the "good cop" tried to convince the criminal he was there to help. In some instances, officers would use the "third degree"—either physical or mental torture—to get the confession they wanted.

The mental torture might include insisting they knew the suspect was guilty and telling the suspect he could go to prison for a long time. It could also include threats of violence. With Miranda, Cooley and Young did not use the third degree. They remained calm, though they never let Miranda know exactly what they already knew about the two crimes.

After the first round of questioning, the officers took Miranda into a lineup room. He and several other men stood on one side of a one-way glass. They could not see through the glass into the room on the other side. Standing behind the glass in that room was Jane Doe. Next to her was Barbara Roe, the victim of Miranda's first crime, a robbery. The two women studied the men in the lineup. They both seemed to think that the first man could have been the criminal, but they were not sure. Man number one was Ernesto Miranda.

When Miranda returned to the sweat room, he asked how he did in the lineup. Cooley answered:

> *Not too good, Ernie.*

The police and Miranda later disagreed on what

happened next. Miranda claimed the officers promised to drop any robbery charges if he confessed to the rape. Cooley and Young denied they made any deals. Whatever happened, Miranda decided to come clean. He admitted he had raped Jane Doe and agreed to sign a written confession.

Ernesto Miranda (far left) was identified by his victims in a police lineup.

Miranda also said that he had robbed Barbara Roe and had tried to rape another woman, but he did not sign confessions for these crimes.

After Miranda confessed, the officers brought Jane Doe into the sweat room. She wanted to hear Miranda's voice so she could identify him without any doubt. He said a few words, and Jane Doe knew he was the one. Barbara Roe also heard him speak and decided he was the man who had robbed her. Finally, Cooley and Young placed Miranda under arrest. He was eventually charged with the kidnapping and rape of Jane Doe and the robbery of Barbara Roe.

Under the U.S. Constitution, all Americans have certain legal rights. They cannot be forced to incriminate themselves or give evidence that might lead to their conviction in a crime. Accused criminals are also allowed to consult a lawyer. During their questioning and arrest of Miranda, Cooley and Young did not mention Miranda's right to remain silent or have an attorney present. Cooley knew Miranda had been convicted of crimes in the past. The officer assumed that Miranda knew all about his rights and chose to give the confession anyway.

The fact that Cooley and Young did not mention Miranda's rights seemed small at the time. The officers were just glad they had found and arrested a possibly dangerous criminal. But as Miranda's case entered the court system, legal experts raised

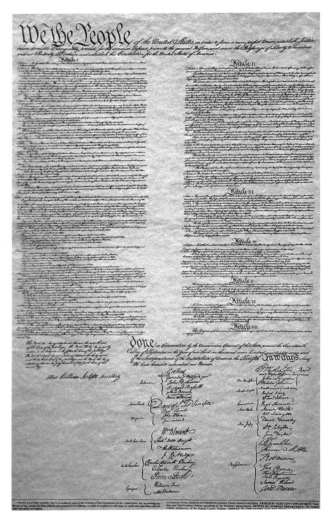

The U.S. Constitution, written in 1787, ensures Americans certain basic rights.

questions about what happened in the Phoenix sweat room on March 13, 1963. Miranda's case would eventually reach the U.S. Supreme Court, the most powerful court in the country. And the court's decision in the case would be one of the most famous in United States history. After the *Miranda* decision, anyone taken into police custody or accused of a crime would first know exactly what his or her legal rights were. ◼

15

The Trials

Chapter

2

When he was arrested in March 1963, Ernesto Miranda was not a stranger to courtrooms and jails. His criminal record started when he was 15 years old. Even before that, he'd had a difficult childhood. Miranda was born in 1941 in Mesa, Arizona. His father had come to the United States from Mexico. When Miranda was 6, his mother died, and his father soon remarried. Miranda did not get along with his stepmother, and he sometimes skipped school. When he did go to class, he often got into trouble. At 14, Miranda finished the eighth grade—his last complete year of formal schooling.

At 15, Miranda was convicted of stealing a car. He was sent to a boys' reform school where he stayed for six months. In January 1956, he was arrested for trying to rape a woman.

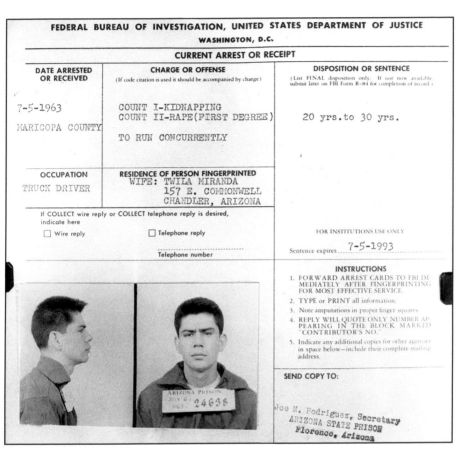

	FEDERAL BUREAU OF INVESTIGATION, UNITED STATES DEPARTMENT OF JUSTICE WASHINGTON, D.C.	
	CURRENT ARREST OR RECEIPT	
DATE ARRESTED OR RECEIVED	CHARGE OR OFFENSE (If code citation is used it should be accompanied by charge)	DISPOSITION OR SENTENCE (List FINAL disposition only. If not now available, submit later on FBI Form R-84 for completion of record.)
7-5-1963 MARICOPA COUNTY	COUNT I-KIDNAPPING COUNT II-RAPE(FIRST DEGREE) TO RUN CONCURRENTLY	20 yrs.to 30 yrs.
OCCUPATION TRUCK DRIVER	RESIDENCE OF PERSON FINGERPRINTED WIFE: TWILA MIRANDA 157 E. COMMONWELL CHANDLER, ARIZONA	

If COLLECT wire reply or COLLECT telephone reply is desired, indicate here

☐ Wire reply   ☐ Telephone reply

Telephone number

FOR INSTITUTIONS USE ONLY

Sentence expires **7-5-1993**

INSTRUCTIONS
1. FORWARD ARREST CARDS TO FBI IMMEDIATELY AFTER FINGERPRINTING FOR MOST EFFECTIVE SERVICE.
2. TYPE or PRINT all information.
3. Note amputations in proper finger squares.
4. REPLY WILL QUOTE ONLY NUMBER APPEARING IN THE BLOCK MARKED "CONTRIBUTOR'S NO."
5. Indicate any additional copies for other agencies in space below—include their complete mailing address.

SEND COPY TO:

Joe M. Rodriguez, Secretary
ARIZONA STATE PRISON
Florence, Arizona

He went back to the boys' school. By the time he was 18, Miranda had been arrested six times. Most of his crimes featured attempted robbery or sexual offenses.

A criminal report described the crimes Miranda was arrested for in 1963.

Miranda then entered the Army, but his problems did not end. He was arrested for being a "peeping Tom"—someone who spies on people inside their homes. The U.S. Army discharged him in July 1959. Miranda then began to steal and sell cars for money. After being caught, he spent almost one year in a federal prison.

Miranda stayed out of trouble for a time, but in 1962, he committed the crimes that led to his arrest in Phoenix the next year. In 1963, when his trials in the *Jane Doe* and *Barbara Roe* cases began, Miranda could not afford an attorney, so the state provided him with one. This lawyer, Alvin Moore, hoped to win his client's freedom by arguing that Miranda was mentally ill. Two doctors examined Miranda, and they found that he had some emotional problems. However, Miranda was not insane by legal standards and would have to face a trial. As one of the doctors told the court:

> *[Miranda] was aware of the nature and quality of his acts and he was aware that what he did was wrong.*

When the Phoenix police arrested Ernesto Miranda, they took his fingerprints.

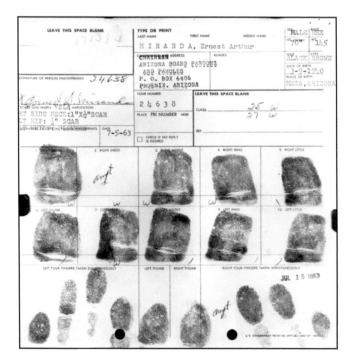

On June 19, 1963, Miranda went on trial for the robbery of Barbara Roe. The first witness was Carroll Cooley, who talked about the day he arrested and questioned Miranda. Moore asked the police officer if he had told Miranda that anything he said could be used against him in court. Cooley said no, and he also admitted that he did not tell Miranda he could have a lawyer present. Moore believed that Miranda's confession was not voluntary—a key point for it to be acceptable in court. Alone in the room with the officers, Miranda might have felt pressured to talk. Judge Yale McFate, however, disagreed. The trial went on, and Miranda was found guilty of robbery.

> ## THE PUBLIC DEFENDER
>
> Alvin Moore was a public defender—a lawyer hired by the state to defend people accused of a crime who cannot afford one. Moore, who was 73 at the time, did not like criminal cases like Miranda's. He felt being around criminals made him think as they did. But Moore felt he had a duty to protect the legal rights of the poor. At the time, other public defenders in Phoenix were refusing to help the poor unless they received more money.

The next day, June 20, Miranda's rape trial began, again with McFate as the judge. Once again, Moore tried to suggest that the confession was tainted, because Miranda's constitutional rights had been denied. He asked Cooley:

> *Did you ever, before or during your conversation or before taking this statement, did you ever advise the defendant he was entitled to the services of an attorney?*

Once again, Cooley said no. Moore asked the judge to throw out Miranda's confession.

19

As part of his objection, Moore said that the U.S. Supreme Court had ruled that accused criminals who were poor could have an attorney present at the time of their arrest. Moore may actually have been referring to a case known as *Gideon v. Wainwright*. This was a case that had just been settled. In *Gideon v. Wainwright*, the U.S. Supreme Court ruled that anyone could have an attorney present during a trial, whether they could afford one or not.

At the time, some states— unlike Arizona—did not provide public defenders to people accused of crimes who could not afford them. But the *Gideon v. Wainwright* decision related to the trial, not to the time of a person's arrest.

Some states did provide an attorney before a trial, but the Supreme Court had never clearly stated that an accused person had the right to have an attorney present while merely being questioned or arrested. Moore had mistakenly argued that the Supreme Court did guarantee that right. McFate overruled Moore's objection. This meant that the jury could consider Miranda's confession when reaching its verdict.

THE FBI AND CRIMINALS' RIGHTS

During the 1940s, one well-known U.S. law enforcement agency began to consider the rights of accused criminals. At that time, officers of the Federal Bureau of Investigation (FBI) would read a statement to suspects of federal crimes. It told them they had a right to remain silent and a right to have an attorney present. Many state and local law enforcement officers, however, had not adopted the use of this statement.

Having failed to get the confession thrown out, Moore ended the case on a weak note. He said Jane Doe had not resisted enough when Miranda tried to rape her. Under Arizona law at that time, a woman was expected to resist fully when being sexually attacked. But Moore's words seemed crude as he tried to blame Jane Doe for the crime. Anything Moore said was unlikely to win Miranda's freedom. Miranda's confession seemed too clear to ignore.

McFate told the jury that if Miranda's confession was voluntary, it could be allowed. And the jury could decide for itself if the confession was voluntary. But, McFate said, the confession could not be considered involuntary just because "a defendant was under arrest at the time he made a confession or that at the time he was not represented by [an attorney], or that he was not told that any statement he might make could or would be used against him."

For five hours that same day, the jury of nine men and three women sat by themselves in a small room to come up with a verdict. They discussed the evidence they had heard. Perhaps most important of all was Miranda's signed confession. Finally, the jury returned to the courtroom with its verdict: guilty of rape and kidnapping. The next week, McFate sentenced Miranda for his robbery conviction and the rape and kidnapping of Jane Doe. For the next 20 to 30 years, Miranda would be behind bars.

After his conviction in 1963, Miranda was sent to Arizona State Prison in Florence, which is still used today.

Alvin Moore was unhappy with the outcome of the two trials. He still believed Miranda's constitutional rights had been denied. In August 1963, Moore appealed the decision. Attorneys make appeals when they believe their clients did not receive fair trials. An attorney might think a judge did not correctly apply the law involved in the case, or that proper rules may not have been followed during the trial.

When an appeal is filed, the case goes to a special appeals court. These courts exist in the federal judicial system, as well as in every state. In the appeals court, the decision reached in the original court, not the crime itself, becomes the focus. The appeals court judges look to see if the judge at the original trial followed proper procedures, as spelled out under existing laws, state constitutions, and the U.S. Constitution.

Moore's appeal meant that the Arizona Supreme Court would hear the facts of Miranda's case. It would decide if the lower court had followed the rules of law in deciding that Miranda was guilty. The state Supreme Court might find that the confession was voluntary and that Miranda had been fairly convicted. Or it might agree with Moore and overturn Miranda's conviction. In the meantime, as the legal process continued, Miranda moved into his new home—a jail cell at the Arizona State Prison. ◣

The First Appeal

As part of the appeals process, Alvin Moore wrote a legal document called a brief. It outlined the details of Miranda's case and why Moore thought the Arizona Supreme Court should overturn the conviction. Moore again said that Miranda had not confessed voluntarily. He asked the justices, or judges, of the court:

> *Was appellant (a Mexican boy of limited education) afforded all the safeguards to his rights provided by the Constitution of the United States and the laws and the rules of the courts?*

Moore clearly thought the answer was no.

The legal appeals process can move slowly, and more than a year passed before Moore was able to present his case to the Arizona justices

in person. During that time, Miranda sat behind bars, hoping to win his freedom. Meanwhile, in Washington, D.C., the U.S. Supreme Court was deciding the case of Danny Escobedo, who had a similar experience to Miranda's. That decision would influence the Arizona justices when they decided Miranda's appeal.

Miranda was confined to a cell in a maximum-security prison, where his movements were tightly restricted.

On the night of January 19, 1960, police in Chicago, Illinois, found the dead body of Manuel Valtierra, who had been shot in the back. The police did not find the gun or other clues, but they knew that in most murder cases, the killer knows the victim. They decided to question Valtierra's wife; her brother, Danny Escobedo; and two of Valtierra's friends. The mother of one of the friends hired a lawyer, who was able to get the four suspects released. Within the next two weeks, the police brought in one of Valtierra's friends a second time. He told them that Escobedo had killed Valtierra.

When the police arrested Escobedo, he said he wanted to talk with his lawyer before answering any questions. The police said no and began questioning Escobedo. Escobedo later said that the officers told him:

> *[You] might as well admit to the crime.*

After hours of questioning, a tired, scared, and tearful Escobedo finally admitted he had been involved in the plot to kill his brother-in-law. He denied, however, pulling the trigger.

At Escobedo's trial, his lawyer argued that the accused's confession should not be allowed as evidence because Escobedo had not been told of his right to remain silent. The judge, however, ignored the request. Escobedo was found guilty of murder and sentenced to 20 years in prison.

He appealed, and the Illinois Supreme Court heard the case in February 1963.

At first, the Illinois Supreme Court threw out the conviction of Escobedo. This was because Escobedo had claimed that the police told him they would not prosecute him if he helped them solve the case. The state of Illinois asked the court to reconsider the case. This time, the justices believed a police officer who testified that no one had made any deals with Escobedo. In its second decision, the highest court in Illinois ruled that Escobedo's statement was voluntary and his conviction should stand.

As a young adult, Danny Escobedo was arrested for several crimes, including the murder of his brother-in-law.

Escobedo had one last chance to escape his prison sentence. His appeals lawyer, Barry Kroll, asked the U.S. Supreme Court to consider the case. Interestingly, this appeal was filed just days after Ernesto Miranda was convicted of his crimes in Arizona. Kroll argued that the police should have granted Escobedo's request to have his lawyer with him during questioning. Without the lawyer present, anything Escobedo said to the police should not have been allowed into the trial.

In June 1964, the Supreme Court reached its decision in *Escobedo v. Illinois*. In a close vote, five justices out of nine agreed with Kroll that Escobedo's constitutional rights had been denied. Justice Arthur Goldberg wrote the decision for the majority. In the decision, Goldberg said that the U.S. Constitution gives the accused the right to have a lawyer present.

Certain conditions, however, would have to be met for this right to apply. Goldberg described these conditions:

The investigation is no longer a general inquiry into an unsolved crime but has begun to focus on a particular suspect, the suspect has been taken into police custody, the police carry out a process of interrogations that lends itself to eliciting incriminating statements, the suspect has requested and been denied an opportunity to consult with his lawyer, and the police have not effectively warned him of his absolute constitutional right to remain silent.

In Escobedo's case, all the conditions outlined by the Supreme Court were met. Escobedo was a "particular suspect" in the killing of his brother-in-law, he had been brought to the police station, and the police had refused to have his lawyer present. The police then prodded him to make incriminating statements without telling him of his right to remain silent. With the Supreme Court's ruling, Escobedo's earlier conviction was overturned.

The Supreme Court ruling stirred debate among legal experts and political leaders. Some people, such as U.S. Senator Barry Goldwater of Arizona, thought decisions such as *Escobedo v. Illinois* gave accused criminals too many rights. Goldwater ran for president in 1964. Although Goldwater lost, he introduced the idea of law and order as a key issue in politics.

LAW AND ORDER

Americans had always sought police protection from criminals. But Senator Barry Goldwater was the first national politician to make law and order a major issue. When Goldwater ran for president in 1964, he often talked about the need to make people feel safe when they left their homes. One way to do this, he believed, was to make sure criminals were arrested and kept behind bars. Goldwater thought the Supreme Court was becoming more concerned with accused criminals' rights than with keeping people safe. Goldwater and others who shared his views wanted to make it easier to convict known criminals. Using their confessions, no matter what, was one way to do that.

The Arizona Supreme Court hears appeals for cases that have been tried in Arizona.

One prosecutor agreed with Goldwater, saying that the Supreme Court's ruling in *Escobedo* "gives the criminal one more advantage." Another warned that one day:

> The Court will rule that we can't talk to a suspect without first giving him a lawyer.

The *Escobedo v. Illinois* decision was a matter of public record when Ernesto Miranda's attorney finally appeared before the Arizona Supreme Court in April 1965. But although the Arizona Supreme Court justices considered the *Escobedo* ruling

CALIFORNIA RULING

Rulings made by the U.S. Supreme Court influence how state and federal courts decide similar cases. A few months after the *Escobedo v. Illinois* decision, the California Supreme Court heard a case called the *People v. Dorado*. Like *Escobedo*, it involved a suspect's right to have an attorney present when being questioned by police. The California justices ruled that police had to inform suspects of their right to have an attorney present. The suspects did not have to specifically ask for a lawyer, as Escobedo had done.

in Miranda's appeal, they rejected the idea that Miranda's case was similar to Escobedo's.

Unlike the Illinois man, Miranda had not asked to have a lawyer present and then been denied that right. Just as Officers Cooley and Young did, the justices assumed that Miranda should have known what his rights were, since he had been arrested several times before. The state Supreme Court said that Miranda's confession was valid even though an attorney was not present. The criminal's constitutional rights had not been denied. This ruling meant that Miranda would remain in jail as a convicted rapist.

Miranda knew he had one last legal hope for release. He sent a petition to the U.S. Supreme Court, asking it to consider the decision of the Arizona Supreme Court. Miranda wrote that he had no money, so he could not pay the $100 fee usually required when petitioning the Supreme Court. Miranda's petition was returned because he had not included all the required legal documents. He sent in a second petition with the proper papers and waited to hear if the Supreme Court would accept his request.

By this time, Miranda's case had caught the eye of Robert J. Corcoran, a lawyer for the American Civil Liberties Union (ACLU). Corcoran thought the Arizona justices had not correctly applied the U.S. Supreme Court's ruling in *Escobedo v. Illinois.* That ruling, he believed, gave a suspect an absolute right to have a lawyer present when they were a "particular suspect." The suspect should not have to ask for a lawyer. But federal and state courts could not agree on this

DEFENDING FREEDOMS

The American Civil Liberties Union (ACLU) was founded in 1920. Its goal is to protect the legal rights spelled out in the U.S. Constitution. ACLU lawyers carefully watch the actions of government officials and study decisions made by the U.S. Supreme Court. Over the years, the ACLU has angered some Americans by supporting unpopular people and positions. For example, some critics have argued that the ACLU cares more about the rights of criminals—such as Ernesto Miranda—than in protecting the victims of crimes. The ACLU argues that constitutional rights apply to everyone, even people who break the law.

right. The matter needed to be settled once and for all. Corcoran found two other lawyers who agreed with his thinking. Attorneys John P. Frank and John J. Flynn said they would help Miranda appeal the Arizona decision to the U.S. Supreme Court.

The American Civil Liberties Union works to protect all Americans from having their rights violated.

Getting to the Supreme Court

While preparing his petition and waiting for the Supreme Court to respond, Miranda learned that two top lawyers were ready to join his legal battle. John Frank and John Flynn worked for one of Phoenix's best law firms. Flynn was an expert in criminal law, while Frank's strength was the U.S. Constitution. Together, they wrote several briefs to send to the Supreme Court, hoping it would hear Miranda's case.

The two lawyers did not think Miranda was innocent. Frank later wrote that he thought Miranda "did something," but he did not know for sure if it was rape. Still, Frank was bothered by the way Miranda's case had been handled. Frank believed Miranda had received a stiff sentence because he had confessed so quickly to the rape of Jane Doe. If a lawyer had been with Miranda in the police station, Miranda might have been charged with a lesser crime. Both lawyers believed that even confessed criminals deserved all the legal protection allowed under the U.S. Constitution.

Flynn and Frank thought the key issues revolved around Miranda's rights under the Fifth and Sixth Amendments to the U.S. Constitution. The Fifth deals with self-incrimination, while the Sixth addresses the right to have an attorney. Although they mentioned the Fifth Amendment in their briefs, their primary argument was Miranda's right to an attorney.

The U.S. Supreme Court building in Washington, D.C., was the site of Miranda's final appeal of his 1963 conviction.

THE FIFTH AND SIXTH AMENDMENTS

The Fifth and Sixth Amendments to the U.S. Constitution contain language that attorneys Flynn and Frank believed related to Miranda's case:

Fifth Amendment

No person shall be held to answer for a capital, or otherwise infamous crime, unless on a presentment or indictment of a Grand Jury, except in cases arising in the land or naval forces, or in the Militia, when in actual service in time of War or public danger; nor shall any person be subject for the same offence to be twice put in jeopardy of life or limb; nor shall be compelled in any criminal case to be a witness against himself, nor be deprived of life, liberty, or property, without due process of law, nor shall private property be taken for public use, without just compensation.

Sixth Amendment

In all criminal prosecutions, the accused shall enjoy the right to a speedy and public trial, by an impartial jury of the State and district wherein the crime shall have been committed, which district shall have been previously ascertained by law, and to be informed of the nature and cause of the accusation; to be confronted with the witnesses against him; to have compulsory process for obtaining witnesses in his favor, and to have the Assistance of Counsel for his defence.

The justices of the Supreme Court had begun to see that the *Escobedo* ruling had created confusion in the U.S. legal system. Some states, such as California, now gave an accused criminal a broad right to have an attorney present at the time of arrest. Ruling on Miranda's case, Arizona had taken a more rigid stand. Since the *Escobedo* decision of 1964, dozens of other cases similar to Miranda's had reached the U.S. Supreme Court. Miranda's petition to the Court arrived in Washington, D.C., in August 1965. A court clerk added it to the growing file of cases related to *Escobedo*.

That November, the nine justices of the Supreme Court met to select the cases they would hear for the coming term. Out of the hundreds they received that summer, the justices decided to hear Miranda's appeal. They grouped it with four other similar cases. All these cases involved the confession of accused criminals who could not afford lawyers. In the Supreme Court, and in history, the cases are known together as *Miranda v. Arizona*.

One of the other cases that was grouped with *Miranda v. Arizona* was *Vignera v. New York*. Michael Vignera confessed to a robbery, but he was never told of his right to have an attorney present. The judge ruled that his confession was still valid, even though Vignera had not been told of his rights.

THE COURT AT WORK

Almost all cases reach the U.S. Supreme Court on appeal from state supreme courts or federal courts. The cases must deal with specific federal laws or the Constitution itself in order for the Supreme Court to consider hearing them. The Supreme Court might decide that a law violates the Constitution and so must not be enforced. When the court makes a decision on a constitutional issue, it remains in effect unless a later Supreme Court decision alters it. A decision regarding a constitutional issue can also be changed with an amendment to the Constitution. Today, the Supreme Court receives about 7,000 petitions per year. It actually hears about 100 of these cases.

37

Another case grouped with *Miranda* was *Westover v. United States*. Carl Calvin Westover had been advised of his rights, but he did not have the money to hire an attorney, and one was not present when he was questioned by both local police and the FBI. The questioning dragged on for 17 grueling hours, and Westover finally confessed to two robberies.

Cases dealing with issues similar to Miranda v. Arizona were heard across the United States.

The third case grouped with *Miranda* was *California v. Stewart*. Roy Allen Stewart was a young African-American. Like Miranda, he had never attended

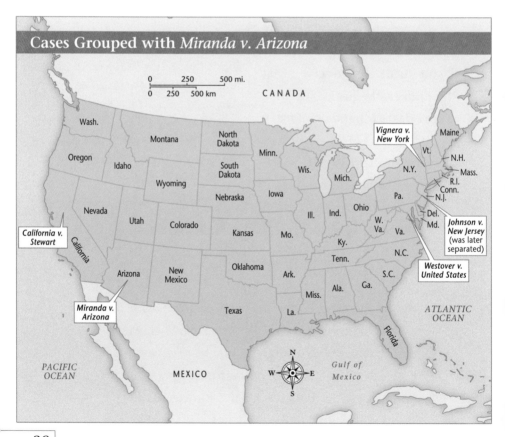

Cases Grouped with *Miranda v. Arizona*

JOHNSON V. NEW JERSEY

In *Johnson v. New Jersey*, the Supreme Court dealt with retroactivity—whether one of its decisions applied to a case that was already settled. The Court decides on its own whether or not a decision is retroactive. *Johnson v. New Jersey* involved two men, Sylvester Johnson and Stanley Cassidy, who had confessed to a murder. They were convicted in 1960—long before the *Escobedo* decision. Johnson and Cassidy argued that the decision in *Escobedo* should apply to their case as well. In its 1966 decision in *Johnson v. New Jersey*, the Supreme Court said *Escobedo* only applied to cases still under appeal at the time of or after the *Escobedo* decision.

high school and had turned to crime early in life. Over a period of five days, police questioned Stewart about his role in a series of robberies and a murder. He finally confessed to robbing a murder victim and was found guilty of robbery and murder. The California Supreme Court overturned the conviction, because he had not been told of his right to remain silent or to have an attorney. The state of California then appealed to the U.S. Supreme Court, hoping the conviction would stand.

The fourth case related to *Miranda* was *Johnson v. New Jersey*. It was later separated from the others and tried separately.

Several months passed before the Supreme Court actually began to consider *Miranda v. Arizona* and the related cases. Frank and Flynn had used that time to work on their brief, which explained the details of the case and the constitutional issues. The Supreme Court received the brief in January 1966. When arguing cases before the

John Flynn (left) represented Miranda, (far right) in front of the U.S. Supreme Court.

Supreme Court, lawyers look for precedents, or decisions made earlier in similar cases. They also often quote the words of past Supreme Court justices to support their views. Frank and Flynn, citing a 1932 case, wrote:

> *[The accused] requires the guiding hand of counsel at every step in the proceedings against him. When Miranda stepped into Interrogation Room 2, he had only the guiding hand of Officers Cooley and Young.*

The state of Arizona responded with its own brief. In it, one of the state's attorneys disputed Frank and Flynn's claim that Miranda was "poorly educated [and] mentally abnormal." The attorney also wrote that the cases of *Escobedo* and *Miranda* were not similar at all. The details

of Miranda's case did not match the guidelines the Supreme Court had set down in its 1964 *Escobedo* decision. Therefore, the attorney argued, the Supreme Court had no reason to overturn Miranda's conviction.

Altogether, the lawyers involved on both sides of the *Miranda* case submitted more than 700 pages of information. The Supreme Court justices then had to read through this huge stack of documents. At the end of February 1966, Miranda's legal team appeared before the Supreme Court to make its oral, or spoken, arguments. What they said would help decide the fate of Miranda and define the legal protection given to all suspects of all crimes. ◢

Inside the Supreme Court

Chapter 5

On February 28, 1966, John Flynn stood in front of the nine justices of the U.S. Supreme Court. The chief justice, Earl Warren, sat in the center of the other eight justices. The justices wore long, black robes—a symbol of their power and importance. The room, too, suggested the power of the court. The space was huge, with ceilings 44 feet (13 meters) high. Oak walls and two dozen marble pillars surrounded everyone in the room. Behind the justices hung a long, red velvet curtain.

The justices had a variety of backgrounds and beliefs. The court's liberals included Chief Justice Warren and Justices William O. Douglas, Hugo Black, and Abe Fortas. They tended to favor protecting individual rights as much as possible. The court's conservatives included

John Marshall Harlan and Byron White. They usually wanted the court to take a limited role in deciding what was constitutional. In criminal cases, they often sided with the government and law enforcement officials. William Brennan, Potter Stewart, and Tom Clark were often swing votes, siding with either the conservatives or the liberals, depending on the case and its constitutional issues.

In 1966, the nine members of the U.S. Supreme Court heard the case of Miranda v. Arizona.

POLITICS AND THE CHIEF JUSTICE

In theory, the justices of the Supreme Court are not involved in politics. They are supposed to make decisions based on the Constitution and legal precedents. But in practice, they often reflect the attitudes of the presidents who named them to the court. In 1953, President Dwight D. Eisenhower named Earl Warren as chief justice. Eisenhower and Warren were both members of the Republican Party. Other Republicans expected Warren to champion their party's values. These included reducing the role of the federal government in business and daily life and limiting the role of the court in overturning laws. Warren, however, upset some Republicans with his decisions. His most famous was *Brown v. Board* of *Education* (1954), which said segregation of whites and African-Americans was illegal. Since Warren, other justices have turned out to be either more liberal or more conservative on the court than they were before joining it.

John Frank was the lead attorney for Miranda, and normally he would have made the oral arguments. But his partner, John Flynn, had spent more time arguing cases in court, and Frank decided he should present Miranda's case. Flynn rehearsed with other lawyers what he would say once in the courtroom. Nevertheless, Flynn said he was terrified when he faced the nine justices to make his oral arguments.

During oral arguments, lawyers have 30 minutes to speak. During that time, they try to make their points as quickly and forcefully as possible, knowing the justices will ask questions along the way. Flynn began by outlining the details of Miranda's arrest and confession. He said that Officers Cooley and Young had not told Miranda he had a right to remain silent and a right to an attorney. Justice Abe Fortas then asked Flynn to clarify that he had said Miranda had not been told he had the right to remain silent. "That is correct," Flynn replied.

Fortas had made a point of addressing the Fifth Amendment issue that Flynn had always thought was part of Miranda's case. Flynn decided he should in fact now shift his focus from the Sixth Amendment to the Fifth as he made his arguments. To him, the two amendments were linked. The right not to speak to police also meant a right to have a lawyer there to help a suspect in police custody. He hoped Fortas and the other justices would agree.

Flynn stressed that Miranda was poor, uneducated, and emotionally unstable. Such a person, he argued, lacked the legal advantages of someone who was wealthy and well schooled. He said:

> *[Those people were] rich enough to hire counsel ... educated enough to know what their rights are ... strong enough to withstand police interrogation and assert their rights.*

In theory, Flynn argued, someone like Miranda already had the same rights as the rich and well educated. But in practice, when crammed into a sweat room with police officers, those rights were not always protected. To protect those rights, police should inform all suspects of them once the suspect was in police custody. Otherwise, Flynn said:

> *[Suspects would be called] upon to surrender a right [they] didn't fully realize and appreciate that [they] had.*

Gary Nelson, the lawyer for the state of Arizona, spoke next. He admitted that suspects should be informed of their rights at some point. But each case would be different as to when that should be. Nelson said giving a suspect the right to a lawyer when merely being questioned would end all questioning. No lawyer would tell clients to speak to the police, even if they were not under arrest.

Duane R. Nedrud was one of several other lawyers who opposed Flynn's argument. He said:

> *I would go so far as to say that I think the state should appoint him a lawyer, if he asks for a lawyer. I do not think, however, that we should in effect encourage him to have a lawyer.*

When Chief Justice Warren asked why not, Nedrud echoed Nelson. A defense lawyer's job is to free a client in any way possible. The lawyer's duty is to "prevent a confession from being obtained." But for police and prosecutors, confessions were usually the best way to convict a criminal.

The oral arguments in the case of *Miranda v. Arizona* stretched over three days. The lawyers in the other cases in the group made points similar to those of Flynn. They referred to earlier cases, such as *Gideon* and *Escobedo*.

Victor M. Earle, the lawyer defending Michael Vignera, noted a warning used by police in Washington, D.C. It told suspects they had a right to remain silent, and if they chose to speak, whatever they said could be used as evidence against them in court.

Earl Warren (1891–1974) served as the chief justice of the U.S. Supreme Court from 1953 to 1969.

The suspects were also informed of their right to have an attorney. If the suspects did not have an attorney, one would be appointed for them when they went to court—but not at the questioning stage. The last point, Earle said, was the only thing that bothered him about the D.C. warning. He believed, as Flynn did, that the suspect had an absolute right to a lawyer while under questioning.

Questioning that view was Thurgood Marshall. At that time, he was the solicitor general—the chief attorney for the U.S. government. He presented the government's argument in *Westover v. United States.* Marshall argued that the federal government did not have the resources needed to provide an attorney to every single person who needed one.

On March 2, 1966, the oral arguments in the case ended. Now it was time for the Supreme Court justices to make their decision. The process would take months, as they weighed the facts of the case.

THURGOOD MARSHALL

Thurgood Marshall played a small part in the *Miranda* case. But he is best known for his legal work before and after *Miranda*. Marshall, the great-grandson of a slave, became a lawyer in 1933. He then worked for the National Association for the Advancement of Colored People, which tried to protect the legal rights of African-Americans. Appearing before the U.S. Supreme Court, Marshall won 29 cases, including the famous 1954 segregation case, *Brown v. Board of Education.* In 1965, he was the first African-American to serve as solicitor general, and two years later he became the first black justice on the Supreme Court. Marshall remained a Supreme Court justice until 1991, two years before his death.

Ernesto Miranda and the other convicted criminals involved in the cases eagerly awaited the Supreme Court's decision. ◣

Thurgood Marshall (1908-1993) was named to the U.S. Supreme Court in 1967.

The Court Decides

Chapter 6

The justices of the U.S. Supreme Court meet privately to discuss each case they hear. They examine the points of law raised in the briefs and oral arguments. In most cases, the Supreme Court reaches a decision in just one meeting, but sometimes the justices meet again. By tradition, the chief justice speaks first, followed by the justice with the most time spent on the court, and continuing in order by time served. When the justices are done discussing, they vote in reverse order: from the junior justice to the chief justice.

Given the secrecy of these meetings, no one knows for sure what the justices said when they decided *Miranda* or when exactly they decided it. All of the justices except Fortas had also heard *Escobedo*. Of those eight, the justices had split in

The scales of justice were first used as a symbol of the legal system thousands of years ago, representing the idea that judges must fairly weigh, or consider, all the facts in a case before making their decision.

that decision. Warren, Douglas, Black, and Brennan had voted to overturn Escobedo's conviction, while Clark, Harlan, White, and Stewart had voted to uphold it. Fortas would likely hold the key vote in this case.

The junior justice, or the justice who had spent the least time on the court, had given some indication of his thinking on the Sixth Amendment in an earlier decision, *Kent v. United States*. Fortas wrote:

> *The right to representation by counsel is not a formality. It is not a grudging gesture to a ritualistic requirement. It is of the essence of justice.*

In the end, Fortas joined the other four justices who had ruled in favor of Escobedo. The majority ruled for Miranda.

Chief Justice Warren wrote the court's opinion, the document that gives the justices' decision and explains why the majority ruled as it did. Working with his clerks, he wrote a first draft of the opinion, and on

OPINIONS OF THE COURT

When the U.S. Supreme Court began in 1789, each justice wrote an opinion for every case. That practice ended during the early 19th century. Now, after the Supreme Court reaches a decision, one justice writes an opinion for the majority. If the chief justice is in the majority, he or she chooses who will write the opinion. If the chief justice is in the minority, the senior member of the majority chooses the writer.

May 18, he sent it to the other justices. The justices in the minority in a Supreme Court decision can write dissents, explaining why they voted against the majority. Justice Harlan let Warren know he would be writing a dissent for *Miranda*, and Clark and White later wrote dissents as well.

Chief Justice Warren wrote notes that he later used when writing the court's decision for Miranda.

53

After reviewing the court's opinion, Justice Brennan suggested not spelling out what rights a person accused of a crime had in the police station and leaving it up to the states to decide. Chief Justice Warren, however, wanted to set a standard for the states to follow and not leave any questions, as the *Escobedo* decision had. Brennan added:

> [Miranda v. Arizona] *would be one of the most important decisions of our time.*

After taking comments from the justices, Warren wrote two more drafts of his opinion before it was final.

In some cases, the Supreme Court merely issues its printed opinion without making any public statements. But Warren, realizing the importance of *Miranda v. Arizona*, decided to read the entire 61-page decision in public. On June 13, 1966, the justices sat in the courtroom as reporters looked on. Warren took almost an hour to read the decision, and at times his voice filled with emotion. When he was done, Americans had new legal protections of their constitutional rights.

Warren began by saying the cases in *Miranda v. Arizona* addressed a core issue of the U.S. justice system. How does the country effectively prosecute criminals while observing the rights protected by the Constitution? As John Flynn had stressed in his oral arguments, Warren saw the key right as the Fifth Amendment—the right against self-incrimination. He noted that suspects, once they are in police custody, face great pressure to speak. Anything they say should not be allowed in court until they are clearly told of their right not to speak and to have an attorney with them.

Warren then examined the history of the legal right against self-incrimination, tracing its roots to old English laws. The government had the duty to produce evidence against an accused criminal. The accused had a right to remain silent throughout a legal investigation and trial. Warren pointed out that protection against self-incrimination currently existed in England, Scotland, and India.

No Cameras Allowed

When the Supreme Court presented its historic decision in *Miranda v. Arizona*, no television cameras broadcast Earl Warren's words. No photographers clicked away, recording the faces of the justices and the others present. The justices of the Supreme Court followed then—and still follow—traditions that do not let any cameras into the courtroom while conducting official business. The media hire artists to sketch the justices and lawyers arguing before them. In recent years, the justices have agreed to release audiotapes of oral arguments in special cases. Federal appeals courts can decide on their own whether or not to let in TV cameras, depending on the case. At the state level, most appeals courts do allow TV cameras to broadcast arguments, and some lower courts do as well.

Newspapers such as The New York Times *reported on the Supreme Court's decision in* Miranda v. Arizona.

HIGH COURT PUTS NEW CURB ON POWERS OF THE POLICE TO INTERROGATE SUSPECTS

DISSENTERS BITTER

Four View Limitation on Confessions as Aid to Criminals

Warren also noted studies that showed some police officers abused suspects in some way to make them confess. He then cited manuals commonly used to train police officers, which stressed the importance of questioning suspects when they are alone.

The goal was to isolate prisoners and make them feel threatened. In that state, they would be more likely to tell officers what had happened—or perhaps even confess to something they did not do, just to end the questioning. Others might make a false confession because they were mentally ill or did not understand what they were doing.

To make sure confessions were valid, Warren said, they had to be voluntary. To help ensure they were voluntary, police had to inform suspects of their rights. In the *Miranda* decision, Warren wrote:

> *[In] none of these cases did the officers undertake ... at the outset of the interrogation to insure that the statements were truly the product of free choice.*

With the *Miranda* decision, the Supreme Court decided that the state or federal government had to provide an attorney if suspects wanted one but could not afford it. Suspects could waive their rights and decide to speak to police without an attorney, realizing what they said could be used against them later in court. However, in court, prosecutors could not use any statements made by suspects who had not been informed of all of their legal rights.

THE BILL OF RIGHTS

The Fifth and Sixth Amendments are part of the Bill of Rights, 10 amendments added to the Constitution in 1791. At the time, some Americans believed the original Constitution did not protect individual's rights against the power of the government. The Bill of Rights was added to spell out extra legal protections. Other key parts of the Bill of Rights are the First Amendment, which guarantees free speech and freedom to worship as one chooses, and the Second Amendment, which protects a person's right to own guns.

When Warren finished with his opinion, each of the four dissenters presented theirs. At times, they also showed great emotion. Justice Harlan's face reddened as he gave his dissent, and at times he pounded his desk. The justice declared that the court's decision would lead to harmful consequences for the country at large.

In general, the dissenters argued that the majority had found a right in the Constitution that did not exist. The Constitution says a person does not have to incriminate himself in court. And the right to an attorney also applies to a trial. Those protections, they exclaimed, do not apply inside a police station.

Harlan noted that the *Miranda* ruling would make it much harder to get criminals to confess. Justice White said that without those confessions:

> *In some unknown number of cases the Court's rule will return a killer, a rapist, or other criminal to the streets and to the environment which produced him, to repeat his crime whenever it pleases him.*

Byron White (1917–2002) served on the U.S. Supreme Court from 1962 to 1993.

That night, Ernesto Miranda watched the television news in the Arizona State Prison. He learned that his appeal had been successful. He would receive a new trial for the rape of Jane Doe. The Supreme Court decision, however, did not affect his conviction for the robbery of Barbara Roe. John Flynn went to work winning a new trial for that case as well. While Miranda remained in prison, his name became famous across the country. Soon lawyers and police officers everywhere were talking about the "Miranda rights" the Supreme Court had outlined. ◣

The Arguments Over *Miranda*

Chapter

7

For many Americans, the *Miranda* decision was a disgrace. Many legal experts and politicians spoke out against it, with concerns similar to those of the dissenting justices. They felt that the number of voluntary confessions would fall, thus reducing convictions. A Texas officer said:

> *We might as well close up shop.*

Maryland's state attorney worried that some criminals waiting for trials would go free because they had given confessions that did not meet the conditions of the *Miranda* ruling. Others said the Supreme Court seemed more concerned with protecting the rights of criminals than the public who suffered from their crimes.

There was a fear among police officers and some Americans that the Miranda ruling would give criminals an advantage.

'WHAT D'YA KNOW – THEY'RE MAKIN' A
POLITICAL ISSUE OF LITTLE OLD ME!'

After the Miranda ruling, political cartoons appeared in newspapers that expressed the view that criminals had been given a huge advantage.

Some police officers thought the court's decision was an insult to them and the hard work they did to win convictions. They believed the decision suggested they lacked the skills to find the guilty and had to force out confessions.

Other officers said they did not understand all the points explaining what they could and could not do before questioning a suspect. In New Haven, Connecticut, law students studied police operations shortly after the *Miranda* ruling. They found that many officers forgot or chose not to tell suspects their rights. In some cases, the police hinted that suspects could face more trouble if they did exercise their rights.

In August 1966, 900 police officers and lawyers met in Michigan to discuss the *Miranda* ruling. Some were angry. Officials from poor cities and counties wondered how they could afford to hire public defenders for accused criminals. But a few police officers almost welcomed the ruling. One told a reporter that experienced criminals and the educated already knew what their rights were.

He said:

> *The only people this really protects are the ignorant, and that's not a bad thing.*

Another officer thought the *Miranda* ruling would force the police to work harder to investigate crimes. They could no longer rely on confessions alone to win convictions.

Whatever their feelings about the *Miranda* ruling, the police knew they had to live with it. In California, the state government's top attorney ordered two prosecutors to write out a short list of the rights the Supreme Court had given in *Miranda*. Police officers would read the rights before questioning a subject. Soon,

THE WRITERS OF THE MIRANDA WARNING

In the summer of 1966, California prosecutors Harold Berliner and Doris Maier spent a few hours writing what is thought to be the first Miranda Warning. Berliner later said, "We ... tried to find practical words to express the court's notion, in language simple enough for an ordinary suspect to understand." Berliner was also a printer, and he printed the warning on plastic cards and began selling them to police departments across the country. A few years ago, Berliner changed the warning. The third sentence now refers to a lawyer as "him or her."

officers across California received a card with instructions on what to tell suspects before beginning questioning.

The sentences that were to be read to the suspect were soon known as the Miranda Warning. Police officers all over the United States began to use the California version of the warning. Americans heard the Miranda Warning on television police shows, such as *Dragnet*. And officers and criminals knew "reading the rights" was an expected part of any arrest. Some officers, however, were unsure when to read the

After the Supreme Court decision, officers across the country began reading suspects of crimes their Miranda rights.

```
┌──────────────────────────────────────────────────────────┐
│ DEFENDANT                    │ LOCATION                    │
│                              │                             │
│                                                            │
│     SPECIFIC WARNING REGARDING INTERROGATIONS              │
│                                                            │
│  1. YOU HAVE THE RIGHT TO REMAIN SILENT.                   │
│                                                            │
│  2. ANYTHING YOU SAY CAN AND WILL BE USED AGAINST YOU IN A │
│     COURT OF LAW.                                          │
│                                                            │
│  3. YOU HAVE THE RIGHT TO TALK TO A LAWYER AND HAVE HIM    │
│     PRESENT WITH YOU WHILE YOU ARE BEING QUESTIONED.       │
│                                                            │
│  4. IF YOU CANNOT AFFORD TO HIRE A LAWYER ONE WILL BE      │
│     APPOINTED TO REPRESENT YOU BEFORE ANY QUESTIONING,     │
│     IF YOU WISH ONE.                                       │
│  SIGNATURE OF DEFENDANT                │ DATE              │
│                                        │                   │
│  WITNESS                               │ TIME              │
│                                        │                   │
│  ☐ REFUSED SIGNATURE   SAN FRANCISCO POLICE DEPARTMENT  PR.9.1.4 │
└──────────────────────────────────────────────────────────┘
```

rights because it was not clear to them when someone was officially in police custody.

With their concerns over *Miranda*, some police departments began to keep track of what happened with confessions and convictions. A study in New York showed a dramatic drop-off in the number of defendants willing to speak to police. However, in Kansas City, Missouri, police noted only a small number of suspects who were now not talking to police. And in California, more felons actually confessed after the *Miranda* ruling went into effect.

Newspapers and magazines also sometimes reported about confessed criminals who went free because of *Miranda*. One of them was a 22-year-old New York man who admitted he had killed his

Police carried printed cards with the Miranda Warning, and some officers had the accused sign the card to verify they had been read their rights.

wife and her five children. In Cincinnati, Ohio, a suspect in a robbery was released and then went out and committed another crime. In California, another confessed murderer who had already been convicted went free.

The *Miranda* ruling also affected America's judges. They now had to put into practice the Supreme Court's opinion. Warren wrote that the Miranda rights applied as soon as someone was brought into custody "or otherwise deprived of freedom of action." Determining what constituted police custody now became a tricky issue, and a number of court cases addressed the issue in the coming years.

For example, in 1971, a New York court ruled that prosecutors could use statements made before a suspect is read his or her rights. These statements could only be used in a court to question a suspect's truthfulness, but not to prove guilt. Several years later, the Oregon Supreme Court said that a robbery suspect lost freedom of action when the suspect agreed to an officer's request to go to the police station. The suspect then gave a confession behind closed doors without being read his rights. The court said he should have received the Miranda Warning. In 1977, the U.S. Supreme Court said the Oregon court had ruled too broadly and overturned the decision.

The questions—and anger—that the *Miranda* decision prompted touched Congress as well. Some of the lawmakers said the Supreme Court had gone too far in protecting criminals at a time when serious crime was on the rise. A few senators held hearings to discuss crime in general and *Miranda* in particular. The lawmakers had legal experts and police officers speak out against the Supreme Court ruling.

In 1968, the opponents of *Miranda* in Congress won a small victory. They passed a crime bill that

Suspects usually knew when they were in police custody, but in some cases involving Miranda rights, the issue was not always so clear.

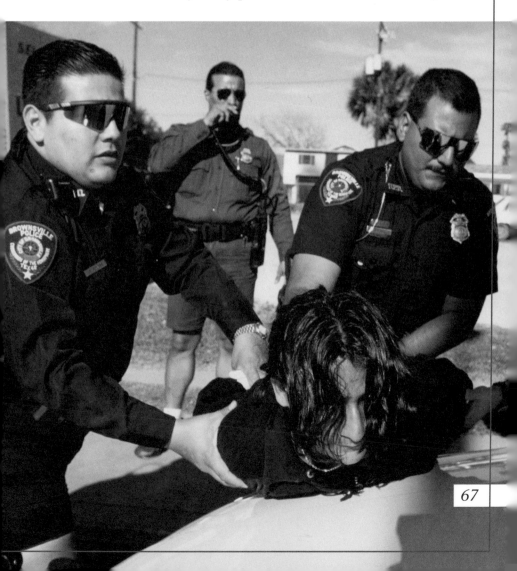

67

included a section on confessions. Section 3501 said that confessions had to be voluntary to be accepted in federal court, but the police's failure to give a Miranda Warning before questioning would not automatically mean the confession was tainted. President Lyndon B. Johnson did not particularly like Section 3501, but he supported the rest of the crime bill. He told federal agents to continue reading suspects their Miranda rights.

Michigan Representative Gerald Ford was a strong backer of Section 3501. He would later become the 38th president of the United States.

In 1968, the same year that Congress passed section 3501, Richard M. Nixon ran for president. Nixon had promised to promote law and order. When speaking to voters, Nixon drew loud cheers when he said:

> *The wave of crime is not going to be the wave of the future in the United States.*

Nixon used the fear of crime and violence to help him win the presidency. The *Miranda* decision had helped make crime and the justice system a key political issue.

But early on, as politicians were just beginning to argue about law and order, Ernesto Miranda was given another day in court. In 1967, he faced a second trial for the kidnapping and rape of Jane Doe. By now, Miranda was a criminal celebrity, since his case had been featured in the news. On both sides, powerful legal figures worked on the new trial. Defending Miranda this time was John Flynn. Robert Corbin, the top prosecutor for the county, argued the case for the state.

Some law-enforcement officers feared the Miranda *ruling would return criminals to the streets to repeat crimes.*

Richard M. Nixon (right) used American voters' fear of crime to help him win the presidency, succeeding Lyndon B. Johnson (left).

Corbin could not use Miranda's sweat room confession of 1963, but Miranda's former girlfriend came forward and testified that Miranda had confessed to her about raping Jane Doe. Based on this evidence, Miranda was convicted again. The result was the same again in 1971,

THE END OF ERNESTO MIRANDA

After his release from prison in 1971, Ernesto Miranda wrote, "I want to obtain an education and to elevate myself in society. I know this will be hard for me, but only at first." Instead, Miranda tried to use his fame to make money. He sold autographed cards of the Miranda Warning at $1.50 apiece. Soon, however, Miranda found himself in legal trouble again. He was arrested for illegally carrying a gun and went back to the Arizona State Prison. In December 1975, he was freed again. Less than a month later, he was playing poker in a Phoenix bar. A fight broke out, and Miranda was stabbed to death. His life was over, but his name lived on in courtrooms across the United States.

when Miranda was tried again for the robbery of Barbara Roe: guilty. Together, he would serve nearly 10 years in prison.

Like Miranda, Michael Vignera, Carl Calvin Westover, and Roy Allen Stewart received new trials after the Supreme Court's ruling on their cases. And like Miranda, each was convicted again for their crimes. Westover received a 30-year sentence, and Stewart was given a life sentence. Vignera, however, had his original sentence reduced from 30–60 years to 7½–10 years. ◣

Miranda Through the Years

8

The 1968 crime bill that tried to weaken the *Miranda* ruling had no real effect. The law only applied to federal law enforcement officials, not state and local police. And even after Richard Nixon replaced Lyndon B. Johnson as president, he let federal officials continue reading the Miranda Warning. Across the country, judges still threw out cases if suspects gave confessions without being told of their Miranda rights. But legal issues related to those rights still reached the U.S. Supreme Court.

Some of these cases placed limits on the Supreme Court's original ruling. In *Harris v. New York*, the Supreme Court ruled in 1971 that a statement taken before a Miranda Warning could be used in court to show a suspect was generally not truthful.

In 1974, the Supreme Court made a major statement about the Miranda Warning in *Michigan v. Tucker*. The case involved what lawyers call "fruit of the poisonous tree." Imagine that a suspect provided information before being read the Miranda rights. That information would help the police find evidence against that suspect.

The evidence is considered tainted because it came from a "poisonous tree"—the statement given before the Miranda Warning was read. Because the evidence—the "fruit"—has the same "poison" as the tree, it should not be allowed in court.

The Supreme Court has continued to make rulings related to Miranda v. Arizona *since its original ruling in 1966.*

The *Tucker* case, like that of *Miranda*, involved a rape. In this case, the defendant was read his rights, but he was not told he would be given an attorney if he could not afford one. By not receiving a complete warning, Tucker's statements were not allowed in court. But something he said in his statement led the police to a witness who made a statement against Tucker. That evidence was allowed in court. Tucker argued that the second statement was the fruit of a poisonous tree.

The Supreme Court decided not to apply the poisonous fruit doctrine to this case. Instead, it looked at the nature of the Miranda Warning.

When the Supreme Court heard arguments in the case of Michigan v. Tucker, *it featured several new members.*

Justice William Rehnquist wrote that the police "had failed to make available the full measure of ... safeguards" connected to self-incrimination. But leaving out part of the Miranda Warning did not mean Tucker's rights had been violated. The Miranda Warning was a tool to protect constitutional rights, not a constitutional right of its own.

After *Tucker,* the court made other decisions that seemed to weaken some of *Miranda's* protections. And some critics of the 1966 ruling still hoped the Supreme Court would overturn *Miranda v. Arizona* altogether. The case that seemed to offer that chance came in 2000: *Dickerson v. United States.*

75

In 1997, the FBI brought Charles Dickerson in for questioning, believing he had taken part in an armed robbery. At the time, he was not under arrest. Like Ernesto Miranda years before, Dickerson believed he had no choice but to go with the agents for questioning. At the office, Dickerson said he had been near the bank, driving a car that witnesses had seen at the time of the robbery. But he denied being involved with the robbery. When the agents told him they were going to get a warrant to search his apartment, Dickerson made a statement indicating he may have been involved in the robbery. The FBI later found evidence, including a gun and money stained with dye, that Dickerson had been involved in a number of bank robberies.

After his conviction, Dickerson appealed. He claimed his rights had been denied because he had not been read the Miranda Warning before making his first statement. A U.S. court disagreed. It pointed to Section 3501 and said that on the whole, Dickerson's statement was voluntary, even if he had not been read his rights. Dickerson then appealed that decision to the U.S. Supreme Court. The Supreme Court decided for Dickerson—and gave the Miranda rights new legal strength.

William Rehnquist was now chief justice, and he wrote the decision in *Dickerson*. He noted that with Section 3501, Congress had tried to overturn the Supreme Court's ruling in *Miranda*. Congress, however, did not have the power to reverse a ruling on a constitutional issue by passing a law. Only an amendment to the Constitution could do that.

William Rehnquist (1924–2005) joined the U.S. Supreme Court in 1972, became chief justice in 1986, and held that position until his death.

Rehnquist pointed to a legal notion called *stare decisis* for the Supreme Court's choosing not to overturn *Miranda*. Stare decisis is Latin for "let the decision stand." It refers to a long tradition in English and U.S. courts. Justices almost always accept the decisions made by earlier courts. At times, courts will ignore precedents or find flaws in them. But with *Miranda*, the Court in 2000 was

willing to accept the decision made by the 1966 court and the later decisions based on *Miranda*. Near the end of his decision, Rehnquist wrote:

> *We do not think there is much justification for overruling* Miranda. Miranda *has become embedded in routine police practice to the point where the warnings have become part of our national culture.*

In 2000, when the Supreme Court upheld the Miranda decision, the nine justices were (from left, standing) Ruth Bader Ginsburg, David Souter, Clarence Thomas, Stephen Breyer, (seated from left) Antonin Scalia, John Paul Stevens, William Rehnquist, Sandra Day O'Connor, and Anthony M. Kennedy.

In the *Dickerson* case, the U.S. Justice Department filed a brief asking the Supreme Court to uphold the *Miranda* decision. The department represented the FBI and other federal law enforcement agencies. Many police officers who at first disagreed with the decision over *Miranda* eventually began to support it. In most cases, the officers gave suspects the Miranda Warning and then found ways to win a conviction. That might mean getting a voluntary confession after suspects waived their rights. Such a confession would be allowed in court. Or the police might find other evidence needed to convict a suspect.

Even though many police had first opposed the Miranda Warning, many have come to see that it did help protect Americans.

With its ruling in *Dickerson*, the Supreme Court made sure *Miranda* would remain in place. But in future cases, the Supreme Court could decide to ignore precedent and overturn *Miranda*, or perhaps weaken it. And the Supreme Court would still hear other issues focusing on the Miranda Warning and Miranda rights.

In 2004, the Supreme Court decided three new cases related to *Miranda*. In one, *United States v. Patane*, the Supreme Court again looked at the issue of fruit from a poisonous tree. This time, the fruit was physical evidence—a gun. The police found the gun based on statements Samuel Patane made before hearing his full Miranda rights. In *Patane*, the Supreme Court decided by a 5-4 vote that the gun could be used as evidence in court.

On the same day it released its *Patane* opinion, the court ruled in *Seibert v. Missouri*. In that case, police arrested Patrice Seibert in the death of her son. Police deliberately did not read her the Miranda Warning before she gave her first statement. They wanted to make her talk as soon as possible and admit guilt, knowing they would read her her rights before doing a second interrogation.

After she admitted a role in her son's death, the police read Seibert her rights, and she agreed to talk without a lawyer present. The Supreme Court ruled that the entire questioning was tainted, because the police had not read Seibert her rights at the beginning.

81

Finally, in *Yarborough v. Alvarado*, the court looked at *Miranda* issues involving the arrest of a teenager, Michael Alvarado. He was convicted of murder based largely on statements he made to police. At the station, the police had refused to let Alvarado's parents stay with him during the questioning, and they did not read Alvarado the Miranda Warning. The lower court said the U.S. legal system often treated juveniles differently than adults. Alvarado should have been considered in custody and been read his rights. The Supreme Court disagreed and overturned the lower court's ruling. The court ruled that Alvarado's age was not a factor in deciding whether he was in custody or not when the questioning began. His conviction stood.

The issue of Miranda rights may come under debate again as the United States tries to prevent terrorist attacks. On September 11, 2001, terrorists killed nearly 3,000 people by crashing planes in

KIDS' RIGHTS

In 1998, Chicago police arrested two boys—7 and 8 years old—for the murder of an 11-year-old girl. They were the youngest ever charged with murder. An officer on the case, James Cassidy, created a new version of the Miranda rights that he read to the boys. He later said, "I wanted to do the right thing," calling his version of Miranda "Kiddie Rights." Cassidy claimed that after he read his version of the Miranda rights, one of the boys confessed. Only later did new evidence show that the boys could not have committed the murder. In 2004 and 2005, the city of Chicago paid the boys and their families millions of dollars for prosecuting them using false evidence.

New York, Washington, D.C., and Pennsylvania. President George W. Bush said his role as commander-in-chief of the U.S. military gave him broad powers to hunt down and imprison terrorists. At times, U.S. citizens accused of being terrorists have not been read their Miranda rights or given their Sixth Amendment right to counsel. The Supreme Court someday may have to decide what role the Miranda rights play in the war on terror.

Prisoners arrested as part of the global war on terror are sometimes not read their Miranda rights.

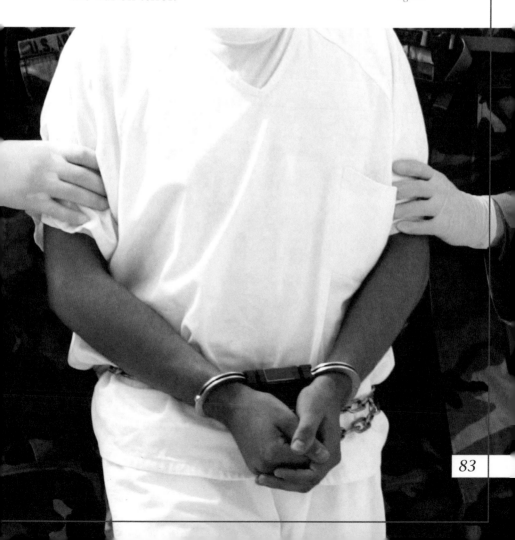

83

Recent debate over Miranda rights has also touched on people who are questioned but not actually brought to trial. In 2002, the U.S. government argued in *Ben Chavez v. Oliverio Martinez* that the issue of whether or not people have been read their rights should only apply if someone is arrested and brought to court. The case involved Oliverio Martinez, who was shot after fleeing from police who wanted to question him. While Martinez was in the hospital, and in great pain, the police questioned him without

Police continue to read the Miranda Warning to suspects taken into custody, even if some legal experts believe it gives criminals too much legal protection.

reading him his rights. Martinez was never tried for a crime, but he sued the officer who shot him, seeking money for having his civil rights denied. The Supreme Court ruled against Martinez, saying that his right against self-incrimination had not been violated.

Some lawyers think the Miranda rights are not perfect. Police officers still have the power to question suspects for hours on end. That long process can wear down people who may be innocent of a crime, leading to a false confession. In some cases, innocent people actually come to believe their own false confession. Some legal experts say the best guarantee of suspects' rights is to videotape all interrogations. Don Rabon, formerly of the North Carolina Justice Department, said:

> *In the investigative process we ought to be ready for the light of day to shine on everything. Techniques we use should not be hidden behind a curtain.*

Confessions will always remain a key part of solving a crime. Juries find a suspect's admission of guilt hard to ignore. But as Miranda's case and others have shown, confessions are not always given freely, or with a suspect knowing their rights under the U.S. Constitution. Since the 1966 *Miranda* decision, Americans have a better understanding of their rights if they are taken into police custody. The Miranda rights remain a key legal protection of their freedoms. ◣

Timeline

December 1791

The Bill of Rights is added to the U.S. Constitution. The Fifth and Sixth Amendments are designed to protect the rights of people accused of breaking the law.

March 1941

Ernesto Miranda is born in Mesa, Arizona.

April 1958

Miranda joins the Army but is discharged about one year later.

December 1959

Police arrest Miranda for stealing a car, and a federal court sentences him to one year in prison.

January 1960

Danny Escobedo is arrested for murder in Chicago, Illinois.

March 1963

Miranda abducts and rapes Jane Doe.

March 1963

Miranda confesses to raping Jane Doe. He is arrested for that crime and the robbery of another woman.

March 1963

In *Gideon v. Wainwright*, the U.S. Supreme Court rules that the state must provide an attorney to people who cannot afford one while on trial.

June 1963

Miranda is convicted of rape and robbery.

July 1963

Escobedo appeals his conviction for murder to the U.S. Supreme Court.

August 1963

Miranda's lawyer, Alvin Moore, appeals Miranda's convictions for rape and robbery to the Arizona Supreme Court.

June 1964

The U.S. Supreme Court decides *Escobedo v. Illinois*, giving suspects the right to have an attorney present during police questioning.

January 1965

In *People v. Dorado*, the California Supreme Court rules that police must inform suspects that they have a right to have an attorney present during questioning.

April 1965

The Arizona Supreme Court rejects Miranda's appeal.

June 1965

Robert Corcoran of the American Civil Liberties Union joins the effort to overturn Miranda's convictions.

August 1965

Miranda petitions the U.S. Supreme Court.

November 1965

The court agrees to hear Miranda's appeal as well as the related appeals of Michael Vignera, Carl Calvin Westover, and Roy Allen Stewart.

January 1966

John Frank and John Flynn, Miranda's new attorneys, submit a brief to the Supreme Court.

February 1966

Oral arguments begin at the Supreme Court for *Miranda v. Arizona*.

March 1966

Oral arguments end for *Miranda v. Arizona*.

May 1966

Chief Justice Earl Warren sends a draft of the opinion for *Miranda* to the other justices on the Supreme Court.

June 1966

Warren delivers his opinion, which rules in favor of Miranda and outlines what are soon known as Miranda rights. Justice John Marshall Harlan delivers a strong dissent in the case.

Summer 1966

Harold Berliner and Doris Maier write the most popular version of the Miranda Warning, which Berliner prints and distributes to police departments across the United States.

March 1967

At a second trial, Miranda is once again convicted of rape.

June 1968

Congress passes Section 3501, a law designed to overturn the *Miranda* decision in federal cases. President Lyndon B. Johnson instructs federal law officials to continue reading suspects their Miranda rights.

Timeline

September 1971

Miranda has a second trial for his robbery charge and is again found guilty.

December 1972

Miranda is released from prison.

June 1974

In *Michigan v. Tucker*, the court rules that the Miranda rights are meant to protect constitutional rights but are not constitutional rights themselves.

January 1976

Miranda dies in a bar fight in Phoenix.

August 1998

To question two young boys about a murder, a Chicago police officer creates what he calls Kiddie Rights, a simpler version of the Miranda Warning. The boys are arrested but are later freed when new evidence shows they did not commit the murder.

June 2000

In *Dickerson v. United States*, the Supreme Court rules that Miranda rights are constitutional rights.

May 2002

In *Ben Chavez v. Oliverio Martinez*, the Supreme Court rules that an officer's failure to read Miranda rights to someone who was not arrested and tried did not violate the man's civil rights.

June 2004

The Supreme Court hears several new cases that deal with Miranda rights. It rules that suspects must be read their rights at the beginning of questioning for any part of their statement to be allowed in court.

ON THE WEB

For more information on *Miranda v. Arizona*, use FactHound.

1 Go to *www.facthound.com*

2 Type in this book ID: 0756520088

3 Click on the *Fetch It* button. FactHound will find Web sites related to this book.

HISTORIC SITE

The Supreme Court
One First St. N.E.
Washington, D.C. 20543

The Supreme Court offers a variety of educational programs, lectures, exhibits, and a theater where a film on the Supreme Court is shown.

LOOK FOR MORE BOOKS IN THIS SERIES

The Collapse of the Soviet Union:
The End of an Empire
ISBN 0-7565-2009-6

Hurricane Katrina:
Aftermath of Disaster
ISBN 0-7565-2101-7

The Little Rock Nine:
Struggle for Integration
ISBN 0-7565-2011-8

McCarthyism:
The Red Scare
ISBN 0-7565-2007-X

The New Deal:
Rebuilding America
ISBN 0-7565-2096-7

Watergate:
Scandal in the White House
ISBN 0-7565-2010-X

A complete list of Snapshots in History titles is available on our Web site: *www.compasspointbooks.com*

Glossary

abductor
someone who uses force to take a person somewhere

appellant
person or group appealing a court's decision

conservative
in criminal cases, likely to give the police and courts powers to convict accused criminals

Constitution
the legal document that describes the basic form of the U.S. government and the rights of citizens

conviction
legal action that says a person is guilty of a crime

counsel
a lawyer

custody
immediate charge and control of a suspect exercised by an authority

doctrine
set of beliefs or rules

federal
relating to the U.S. government

felon
criminal convicted of severe crimes, such as murder, rape, and armed robbery

incriminate
show proof of a person's role in a crime

junior
person in a group with the least experience

juvenile
person under 18 years of age

liberal
in criminal cases, likely to protect the rights of the accused

object
strongly oppose a legal ruling

parole
release from prison after serving less than the original sentence

petition
document that asks a court to consider an appeal, or the act of sending that document to the court

prosecute
present evidence in court to prove someone's guilt

segregation
policy of keeping people apart, based on their race

suspect
person who may have committed a crime

tainted
spoiled or not good in some way

verdict
decision reached by a jury in a trial

waive
give up or ignore

Source Notes

Chapter 1

Page 8, line 9: Liva Baker. *Miranda: Crime, Law and Politics.* New York: Atheneum, 1983, p. 3.

Page 10, line 24: Ibid., p. 12.

Page 12, line 27: Gary L. Stuart. *Miranda: The Story of America's Right to Remain Silent—.* Tucson: University of Arizona Press, 2004, p. 8.

Chapter 2

Page 18, line 13: Ibid., p. 9.

Page 19, line 25: *Miranda: Crime, Law and Politics*, p. 23.

Page 21, line 15: *Miranda: The Story of America's Right to Remain Silent*, p. 21.

Chapter 3

Page 24, line 8: "Miranda v. Arizona—The Crime That Changed American Justice." *Courtroom Television Network.* 31 Jan. 2006. www.crimelibrary.com/notorious_murders/not_guilty/miranda/5.html

Page 26, line 19: *Miranda: The Story of America's Right to Remain Silent*, p. 35.

Page 28, line 22: *Escobedo v. Illinois.* FindLaw. 31 Jan. 2006. http://caselaw.lp.findlaw.com/scripts/getcase.pl?court=US&foo=oyez&vol=378&invol=478&friend=oyez

Page 30, line 2: "Confessions from Suspects." *Time.* 3 July 1964. 31 Jan. 2006. www.time.com/time/magazine/0,9263,7601640703,00.html

Page 30, line 5: *Miranda: Crime, Law and Politics*, p. 34.

Chapter 4

Page 34, line 12: Ibid., p. 66.

Page 40, line 6: "Miranda v. Arizona—The Crime That Changed American Justice."

Page 40, line 14: *Miranda: The Story of America's Right to Remain Silent*, p. 47.

Chapter 5

Page 45, line 6: *Miranda: Crime, Law and Politics*, p. 132.

Page 45, line 21: Ibid., p. 138.

Page 46, line 4: *Miranda: The Story of America's Right to Remain Silent*, p. 58.

Page 46, lines 18 and 26: *Miranda: Crime, Law and Politics*, p. 141.

Chapter 6

Page 52, line 11: *Kent v. United States.* FindLaw. 31 Jan. 2006. http://caselaw.lp.findlaw.com/scripts/getcase.pl?court=us&vol=383&invol=541

Page 54, line 8: Bernard Schwartz. *Super Chief, Earl Warren and His Supreme Court: A Judicial Biography.* New York: New York University Press, 1983, p. 529.

Page 56, line 19: *Miranda v. Arizona.* FindLaw. 31 Jan. 2006. http://caselaw.lp.findlaw.com/scripts/getcase.pl?navby=CASE&court=US&vol=384&page=436

Page 58, line 4: Ibid.

Chapter 7

Page 60, line 8: "New Rules for Police Rooms." *Time.* 24 June 1966. 31 Jan. 2006. www.time.com/time/archive/preview/0,10987,835800,00.html

Page 63, line 10: "Learning to Live with Miranda." *Time.* 5 Aug. 1966. 31 Jan. 2006. www.time.com/time/archive/preview/0,10987,836154,00.html

Page 63, sidebar: Blair Anthony Robertson. "No One Wants to Hear His Words: How Ex-DA Wrote Miranda Warning." *The Sacramento Bee.* 9 July 2000. 31 Jan. 2006. http://sacbee.com/static/archive/ourtown/history/miranda.html

Page 66, line 10: Ibid.

Page 68, line 18: *Miranda: Crime, Law and Politics*, p. 186.

Chapter 8

Page 71, sidebar: "Miranda v. Arizona—The Crime That Changed American Justice."

Page 75, line 2: Ibid.

Page 79, line 4: *Dickerson v. United States.* FindLaw. 31 Jan. 2006. http://caselaw.lp.findlaw.com/scripts/getcase.pl?court=us&vol=000&invol=99-5525

Page 82, sidebar: Carlos Sadovi. "Harris Case Cop Believes Boy Didn't Know Rights." *The Chicago Tribune.* 23 Aug. 2005, Section 2, p. 1.

Page 85, line 17: Steve Irsay. "Fear Factor: How Far Can Police Go to Get a Confession?" *Courtroom Television Network.* 31 Jan. 2006. www.courttv.com/archive/movie/crowe/fear.html

Select Bibliography

Baker, Liva. *Miranda: Crime, Law and Politics.* New York: Atheneum, 1983.

Hall, Kermit L., ed. *The Oxford Companion to the Supreme Court of the United States.* New York: Oxford Press, 1992.

Leo, Richard A., and George C. Thomas III, eds. *The Miranda Debate: Law, Justice, and Policing.* Boston: Northeastern University Press, 1998.

Schwartz, Bernard. *Super Chief, Earl Warren and His Supreme Court: A Judicial Biography.* New York: New York University Press, 1983.

Stuart, Gary L. *Miranda: The Story of America's Right to Remain Silent.* Tucson: University of Arizona Press, 2004.

Further Reading

Compston, Christine L. *Earl Warren: Justice for All.* New York: Oxford University Press, 2001.

Dupont, Ellen. *The United States Justice System.* Broomall, Pa.: Mason Crest Publishers, 2003.

Horn, Geoffrey M. *The Supreme Court.* Milwaukee: World Almanac Library, 2003.

LeVert, Suzanne. *The Constitution.* New York: Benchmark Books, 2003.

Price Hossell, Karen. *The Bill of Rights.* Chicago: Heinemann Library, 2004.

Wice, Paul B. *Miranda v. Arizona: "You Have the Right to Remain Silent—."* New York: Franklin Watts, 1996.

Index

About the Author

Michael Burgan is a freelance writer for both children and adults. A history graduate of the University of Connecticut, he has written more than 90 fiction and nonfiction books for children. He specializes in U.S. history. Michael has also written news articles, essays, and plays. He is a recipient of an Educational Press Association of America award.

Image Credits

American Civil Liberties Union p. **33**; Arizona State Library, Archives and Public Records, Archives Division, Phoenix pp. **11**, **13**, **6** and **17**, **18**, **22**, **86** (top right and bottom); Corbis pp. **27**, **40–41**, **43**, **47**, **49**, **58**, **65**, **74–75** (Bettman), **30–31** (Richard Cummins), **64** (Kim Kulish), **67** (Najlah Feanny), **73** (Ken Cedeno), **77** (Brooks Kraft), **78–79** (Jason Reed, Reuters), **80** (Joseph Sohm, ChromoSohm Inc.), **83** (Mark Wilson, Pool, Reuters); iStock pp. **5, 25, 88** (Adam Booth), **2, 51, 87** (left) (Mark Evans), **61, 84, 87** (right) (Frances Twitty), **69** (Ryan KC Wong); New York Times p. **56**; Phoenix Police Museum p. **9**; Topfoto p. **15, 86** (top right) (The Image Works); United States Library of Congress pp. **53, 62**; United States National Archives and Records Administration p. **70**; UPPA p. **35** (Photoshot).